*"She's a fantastic l[...] [...]rs love
playing for her and w[...] ,out with her."*
– Lisa Keightley, former Australian cricketer
and England women's cricket coach
(*The Cricketer*, February 2021)

First published in Great Britain 2024 by Red Shed, part of Farshore

An imprint of HarperCollins*Publishers*
1 London Bridge Street, London SE1 9GF
www.farshore.co.uk

HarperCollins*Publishers*
Macken House, 39/40 Mayor Street Upper,
Dublin 1, D01 C9W8

Red Shed is a registered trademark of HarperCollins*Publishers* Ltd.

Copyright © HarperCollins*Publishers* Limited 2024

Cover illustration by Carl Pearce.

ISBN 978 0 00 860889 7

Printed and bound in the UK using 100% Renewable Electricity at CPI Group (UK) Ltd.

001

A CIP catalogue record for this title is available from the British Library.

All rights reserved. No part of this publication may be reproduced,
stored in a retrieval system, or transmitted, in any form or by any means,
electronic, mechanical, photocopying, recording or otherwise, without
the prior permission of the publisher and copyright owner.

Stay safe online. Any website addresses listed in this book are correct at the time of going to print.
However, Farshore is not responsible for content hosted by third parties. Please be aware that online
content can be subject to change and websites can contain content that is unsuitable for children.
We advise that all children are supervised when using the internet.

Some conversations in this book have been fictionalised, however these are based on
real life events using sources from the public domain including video and newspaper
interviews, video footage and written accounts. Every effort has been made to
avoid misrepresenting the events portrayed in this book.

MIX
Paper | Supporting
responsible forestry
FSC™ C007454

This book contains FSC™ certified paper and other controlled
sources to ensure responsible forest management.

For more information visit: www.harpercollins.co.uk/green

HEATHER KNIGHT

Written by Clive Gifford

RED
SHED

★ CHAPTER 1 ★

First in All Formats

"C'mon, Trev!"

Heather 'Trev' Knight walked out onto the green sun-dappled turf at the Manuka Oval cricket ground in Canberra, Australia. A gentle breeze ruffled the flags flying on the boundary. The scenic ground was ringed by oak, elm and poplar trees. It was a lovely place to be and a glorious day for batting – but Heather was walking out into the middle of a World Cup crisis.

Three days earlier, England had suffered a bruising defeat in their opening game of the 2020 Women's T20 tournament. This competition featured the world's best women's national teams in matches lasting twenty overs a side. England had scored 123 runs against the South Africans and felt it was not quite enough. Heather's contribution had been a scratchy six runs from 14 balls before opposing captain, Dane van Niekerk, had got her out.

In reply, van Niekerk and Marizanne Kapp took South Africa into the nineties before both were out and the scoring rate slowed. With three overs to go, South Africa still needed 33 runs, but just as Heather and her teammates thought they might triumph, a couple of towering sixes saw the South Africans win with only two balls left.

Heather hadn't slept well after that loss. As captain of the team, her mind was racing. "You can find yourself stewing after these close games – I've already found fifteen runs we could have saved in the field in multiple ways," she wrote in her BBC Sport blog in February 2020.

She knew there was no need to panic but another defeat could see England exit the tournament early.

The Thailand team England were facing at Manuka possessed some dangerous players. Their veteran all-rounder, Nattaya Boochatham, had taken more T20 international wickets (40) in 2019 than any other player. Each wicket had cost her team just 6.17 runs. Getting past her and her leg spinning teammate, Suleeporn Laomi (who had taken 37 T20 wickets herself in 2019) was not going to be easy.

Still, as number four in a strong batting order, Heather had hoped to put her feet up and watch her team's openers, Amy Jones and Danni Wyatt, build a big partnership. There was even the buffer of the supremely talented Nat Sciver-Brunt at number three. Surely, the captain could sit back and enjoy the view?

Not a chance.

Nattaya Boochatham skipped in to deliver

the second ball of the match, and this wicked delivery beat Amy Jones' swish of the bat. Quick as a flash, wicketkeeper Nannapat Koncharoenkai gathered the ball then swept her hands leftwards to deftly knock the bails off the stumps. Amy was out of her ground. OUT! Stumped! England were 0 for 1.

In the next over, Thailand struck again. Danni Wyatt tried to drive but sliced the ball in the air. Wongpaka Liengprasert, fielding at cover point, had to dive full stretch but securely clasped the dipping ball. The Thai team yelled in delight.

OUT!

"Thailand, brilliant in the field. England, two down!" roared the TV commentator. England were 7 for 2 and in trouble.

Heather was ready for action, with her dark blue pads already strapped on, and her bat and helmet in her hand. Just as well, as she was needed right now to stop an embarrassing slide.

Boosted by taking Danni Wyatt's wicket, Soraya Lateh bounded in enthusiastically – but her bowling was wayward. Heather had to reach for a wide ball but knocked it away for a single. Using her expert hand-eye coordination and all her experience, she kept striking singles. However, when a loose ball was bowled, she tried to hit it to the boundary.

She struck fours in the fourth, fifth and sixth overs, then a pair of wonderful strokes for two more fours in the seventh over.

Out on the grassy banks, England supporters yelled encouragement.

"C'mon, Heather. You can do it!"

"Trev is ticking. She's playing really well."

"Go Heather, go England. We need 150!"

It was the fourth time Heather had played at Manuka, located just outside Australia's capital city of Canberra. On her previous three visits she had scored 51 and 78 versus Australia, and 67 runs versus India, so the ground had good memories for her. At the other end, Nat Sciver-Brunt was also scoring freely as England began building a good total.

Disaster nearly struck in the 13th over, though. Nat advanced down the pitch for a quick run.

"No!" Heather shouted, sending her back as the Thai fielders swooped.

Nat had to dive into her crease to avoid being run out. Phew! Heather looked down the pitch. Her expression seemed to say "Let's do nothing reckless", but then the opposite happened.

As the next ball was bowled, Heather stepped across the line and hit a powerful sweep shot. Up and over the boundary it went for the first six of the day. That took Heather past 1,000 runs in T20 internationals. The crowd applauded. A single off the next ball brought up her half century for the match.

Nat and Heather accelerated. After a good start, the Thai bowlers struggled to contain

Heather as she raced into the sixties, then seventies, then eighties. The scorers in the pitch's famous century-old manual scoreboard (named the Jack Fingleton scoreboard) had their work cut out to keep the board updated by hand as Heather hit two more sixes and 13 fours.

Fans were chattering and cheering in the stands. The crisis was over and England were on their way to a formidable total. Could Heather do something special and score a century? With so few balls to face, scoring a hundred in T20 internationals is never easy. Only two English women had done it before, and both were in Heather's team – Tammy Beaumont and Danni Wyatt.

Heather blotted thoughts of her own score from her mind and focused on facing each ball. She unveiled delicate sweeps and glances, as well as powerful drives and cut shots as she struck the ball to all parts of the ground. She had used many of these shots to score epic centuries in Test matches and One Day Internationals (ODIs) before. Could she do it in a T20 today?

Heather suffered a scare on 95 when Thailand thought they had her out, leg before wicket (LBW) and called for a review. However, the review showed Heather was safe. She swept a single then drove the next ball for another.

With her score on 98, Chanida Sutthiruang bowled a wide ball . . .

Heather rocked back and swung her bat . . .

THWACK!

The ball sped towards the point boundary.

"Two!" Heather sprinted forward, touched her bat down at the other end of the pitch and turned to run back.

The Thai fielder gathered and threw the ball in but Heather was safely in her ground. She held her helmet and bat aloft and turned to accept the applause from the appreciative crowd.

"A first international T20 hundred for the

England captain. She loves this ground," said
ex-England cricket captain Nasser Hussain on
the TV commentary. "The loss against South Africa
a distant memory. She has had some fun in the
sun today . . . It's been a joy to watch."

Heather was buzzing, and to celebrate she
hit the next ball for a monstrous six down the
ground. A thumped two off the last ball meant
that England had scored 176 runs – 108 of which
came from Heather's bat. Her century had
been scored in just 63 balls. Extraordinary!
And her 169 partnership with Nat was the
biggest in T20 World Cup History. Incredible!

Heather had also become the first English
batter *and* the first female cricketer from
anywhere in the world to score a hundred
in all three formats of international cricket:
Test matches, ODIs and T20s, joining other
greats of the game like India's Rohit Sharma
and Brendon McCullum from New Zealand.

"I don't often score quicker than Nat," joked

Heather at the post-match ceremony after England won by 98 runs. "I like batting at Canberra, I think it suits my game."

To prove her point, Heather was back in action two days later at the Manuka Oval, where she top scored again. This time she made 62 not out as England comfortably defeated Pakistan.

What made a shy girl from Devon become such a run machine in international cricket? How did she become captain of the England women's team and star in games all over the world?

It all started many years earlier when Heather wanted to join in with her brother . . .

⭐ CHAPTER 2 ⭐

Trev and Tres

Heather Clare Knight was born in the Lancashire town of Rochdale, near Manchester, on Boxing Day, 1990. She was the second child of Rebecca (Beccy) and Mike; her brother, Stephen, was two years older. When Heather was two, her parents made a big move southward to Plymouth, a city on the southwestern coast of England.

Beccy and Mike bought a house on the outskirts of the city, which left them so short of money that at first they couldn't fully furnish their home. In an interview with the *Times* in July 2016, Heather said, "My dad always bores me with stories about how [. . .] he and my mum used to live off dhal and had deckchairs in their living room."

As a typical younger sister, Heather used to follow her brother around and want to do what he was doing. For a while, she had a fascination with building blocks and making models. Football was also a passion and she joined the Women's Academy at professional football club, Plymouth Argyle. But when Stephen got interested in cricket . . . so did Heather.

Stephen started playing around the age of eight or nine in the Colts team of nearby Plymstock Cricket Club. Their dad would take both children down to the ground. As Stephen played his game, Mike would stand on the boundary showing Heather how to hold a bat and hit a ball.

Interviewed for the *Wisden* cricket website in July 2016, (*Wisden* is an annually published cricket reference book), Heather said, "I've always been quite a competitive character and I enjoy things I'm quite good at. I found I was OK at whacking and catching a ball."

Some of Heather's early cricket education happened at home. Brother and sister would play cricket whenever and wherever they could. She added in her *Wisden* interview, "When my parents were away, Steve and I would play in the house or in the garden and break a few garden chairs. Mum would never be too happy about that."

When Heather was eight, she followed her brother into the Under-9s Colts at Plymstock. She played her first game with a hard ball a year later. All the other players were boys – not that it put her off. In fact, Heather took two wickets in a row with her bowling. In the *Wisden Cricketers' Almanack* 2018, she said, "It was filthy seamers back then, not filthy off-spin. It gave the boys a bit of a shock and I absolutely loved it."

Heather enjoyed her days at Elburton Primary School, close to where the Knight family lived. One of the teachers there ran a school cricket club. Heather joined up in Year Five, not bothered that she was the only girl.

Heather never saw anything odd about girls wanting to play sport and compete. It seemed completely natural to her, and for that, she had her mum to thank. When they were young, Beccy Knight would often take Heather and Stephen down to the local park and whilst they mucked around, she ran laps of the park. Heather's mum was also a demon squash player. "I used to love watching her take down absolutely anyone on a squash court," Heather recalled in her BBC Sport blog in June 2016.

Women's cricket was barely seen or talked about in the 1990s. It was rarely shown on television or written about in the newspapers. Heather didn't even know there was an England women's team until she was in her mid-teens.

In the same blog, Heather also admitted, "I couldn't name one female international cricketer at that stage, and it was from the men's game that I sought my role models."

Trev and Tres

England batter Michael Atherton became
an inspiration, but her first cricketing idol was
a local hero – the attacking Somerset and
England left-handed batter, Marcus Trescothick.
He was nicknamed 'Tres', or sometimes 'Banger'
for his love of sausages, not for his habit of hitting
the cricket ball *really* hard, which he did all
the time. Heather earned her own nickname,
'Trev'. It stemmed from when she was 13
and attended a cricket camp. When she
introduced herself, everyone else thought
she'd said 'Trevor' not 'Heather'. Trevor was
shortened to Trev, and stuck.

As Heather grew older, she moved schools
from Elburton to Plymstock School on Church
Road. It was a short trot down Church Road,
straight over the junction and along the edge
of Dean Cross Park to the entrance of Plymstock
Cricket Club. This was handy for Heather as
she followed her brother up through the ranks
of the youth teams at Plymstock.

Despite being the only girl in an all-boys side, Heather never had any trouble with the players in her own team. They liked Heather, her enthusiasm and her skill as a young cricketer. They made her feel welcome, and treated her like everyone else.

But some players in other teams weren't so respectful. She was called 'sweetheart' and mocked by opponents. At some away games she had to change beforehand or find a loo as there were no female dressing rooms. In an interview with the *Sunday Times* in June 2019, she said, "I got changed in a lot of club toilets. I just got on with it, though."

"I took particular satisfaction in a Sunday friendly match when I was about 13," Heather recalled in a December 2021 video interview on the England and Wales Cricket Board (ECB) website. "An adult male bowler on the other side asked me, 'Do you do the lads' ironing after you've finished play?'"

Heather responded not by getting angry, but

by getting even in the best possible way – by playing winning cricket. "I think I hit 70 odd and whacked him all over the place. I never wanted to be different, I just wanted to be part of the team."

Heather was 14 when she started to play girls' cricket. She was selected to play in the Under-15 Women's County Championship for Devon. She top-scored or joint top-scored in all the games she played for the side in 2004. Admittedly, in one match, she only scored nine not out, but that was enough as Devon had bowled their opponents Dorset all out for just 17 runs!

The following year, Heather was promoted from the Under-15s to the adult Devon women's team. In her second game versus Dorset, only one of the first eight Devon batters scored more than five runs, and that was Heather with a massive 83 that guaranteed victory.

In the next game, she went one better, carving out a brilliant 112 runs in a way her idol

Marcus Trescothick would have been proud of. That wasn't all. When the Devon women's team fielded, Heather bowled five overs, taking four wickets for only 11 runs as Devon crushed Wiltshire. Incredible!

At the same time as she starred for Devon Women, Heather kept on playing for Plymstock's boys' and men's teams. In an interview with the *Guardian* in February 2015, she said, "It really challenged me [. . .] and gave me a good standard of cricket." She was eventually promoted to opening the batting in Plymstock's men's first team, joining her brother Stephen in the side.

In an interview with the *Times* in February 2021, Heather recalled an early game she played for the first team. Heather was opening the batting when Steve came out to bat alongside her. When he heard some of the sexist abuse aimed at his sister from a man fielding in the slips, he wanted to respond angrily. Heather waved him away. She was used to it and had the perfect response. When the next ball was bowled, she launched it for six runs over the square leg boundary.

"I didn't hear much from the slips after that," she chortled.

★ CHAPTER 3 ★

West Country Cricket

Things were getting hectic for Heather. She was studying hard at school and playing as much cricket as she could. At 16, she even found the time for a part-time job in a Plymouth care home in the kitchens, making meals for the residents.

In May 2008, Heather became the first woman to open the batting for a Devon League men's team when Plymstock played Shobrooke Park. She only made two before being bowled. Never mind. There was plenty more cricket to come. Two days later, she was opening the batting in the Women's County Championship for the very first time. Awesome.

The game was played at Harewood Park in Plympton, just up the road from where she lived.

The 2008 championship was a 50-over-per-side competition with the counties split into four top divisions. Below them were four regional divisions, each known as Division Five. Heather's county, Devon, were in Division Five, South & West, which included Gloucestershire, Cornwall, Oxfordshire and Dorset.

Heather made an excellent debut at Harewood Park playing against Cornwall Women. First, she bowled ten miserly overs, costing only 16 runs and taking two wickets. Great! Then, when it was Devon's turn to bat, she top scored with 56 before being beaten by a ball from Nicole Edwards and stumped by the wicketkeeper. However, Devon won the game and were well on their way to a successful season.

Heather had five innings for Devon in the championship and made them all count.

She top-scored again, this time versus Dorset with 74 and took one wicket as Devon won again. Against Oxfordshire, her batting was off the scale. She scored a monstrous 190 off of 148 balls. Heather's knock included 116 runs in boundaries (29 fours)! Devon made 297. In reply, Oxfordshire crumbled and were all out for just 65.

In an interview with the *Cricketer* many years later, in January 2022, Heather reflected on how she was able to build long innings at a young age. "One of my strengths has always been my mental resilience and being able to grit it out and concentrate for long periods of time."

All her hard work was paying off. Devon won their division and Heather topped the women's county cricket run-scoring table with 402 runs. These had been scored at an average of 80.4 runs each time she batted. Below her in the table from other divisions was another young future England star, Danielle 'Danni' Wyatt, on 252 runs, and an already established England batting legend, Clare Taylor, on 244.

Devon were promoted and played the 2009 season in Division Three. Despite competing against tougher opponents, Heather continued to flourish. She was becoming more and more skilled at facing different types of bowlers. She loved the challenge of trying to figure out how to score, however the opposition captain decided to distribute the fielders around the pitch.

Heather also enjoyed travelling to new places, because playing in Division Three meant trips further afield, including Derbyshire and up to Edinburgh to play the Scotland women's team. Heather had a brilliant time in both places, scoring 100 not out in the Scottish capital, Edinburgh, and a brilliant 129 in Derby – an innings which included 19 fours and two sixes. In both games, Heather guided Devon to wins.

Her county finished the season in second place, an agonising one point behind Worcestershire. But Heather topped the county championship run-scoring table again, this time with 622 runs. Second in the table on 491 runs was none other than Charlotte Edwards, who was England Women's captain at the time.

Heather was a sought-after player in women's cricket. However, Devon weren't in the top divisions, so Heather had to switch counties to progress. It was hard, but she knew she had to give herself the best possible chance to succeed. In 2009, she began playing club cricket for Reading Women in the Women's Premier League, and a year later, was playing for Berkshire.

Amongst her new teammates at Reading and Berkshire was Isa Guha, an England star and the world number one ranked ODI bowler at the time. Heather, though, wasn't fazed by big names, either in her team or in the opposition. She wanted to learn from and compete against the best players possible.

In her first league season with Reading, Heather blazed 95 against Hayes Hurricanes,

61 versus Gunnersbury Women and 69 versus Brighton and Hove Women. She took three wickets against Bath: two bowled and one caught (by Isa) to help her team win again. Reading won seven of their ten games to finish second in the league table.

Heather still lived in Plymouth and played men's cricket in Devon each Saturday. Then, she'd travel 300 kilometres to London for a game with her new teams on Sunday before heading 300 kilometres back. Heather had her parents to thank for ferrying her back and forth each weekend; Beccy and Mike spent a *lot* of time driving.

"I'd revise for my exams in the car," Heather recalls in an April 2018 article on cricketing website ESPNcricinfo. "Then on Monday I'd go to school, and my parents would go to work. They didn't have much of a social life."

All the travel, hard work and constant cricket was paying off. Heather was invited to join the

England Academy, which strived to develop the next generation of international cricketers. She played a five-match series for the England Academy versus a Europe Women's side, scoring 103 in one game and batting alongside Tammy Beaumont and Danni Wyatt.

That five match series and a couple of September games for Devon Women were it for Heather cricket-wise in 2009. It would be all change for her as she was moving away from home. Heather Knight was off to uni!

★ CHAPTER 4 ★

From Student to Debut

"And on your left is the famous painting of medieval Florence by Jane Eleanor Benham Hay, completed in 1867 . . . "

Heather gazed at the ancient arched windows and famous artworks. She was in the monumental Great Hall of Homerton College in Cambridge on a tour round its ornate buildings, its orchard and its croquet ground.

Heather had managed to balance her cricket and studies successfully. She loved science, particularly biology, and was expecting good grades. As a result, she was offered a prized place to study natural sciences at Cambridge University.

She was well aware of Cambridge's reputation and the sorts of famous scientists and artists it had produced over the years. But she turned down the place there in favour of going to Cardiff University. In an article in the *Independent* from July 2015, she said, "I knew that I wanted to play for England – that was my dream – and I knew that it would be harder to achieve that dream if I went to Cambridge."

Cardiff had an impressive bioscience department and an MCC (Marylebone Cricket Club) University cricket academy, one of just six in the UK. Both appealed to Heather when she visited on an open day.

Heather enjoyed her time in Cardiff. When not in class or playing cricket, she enjoyed cycling around the Taff Trail, hiking up the hills of the Brecon Beacons or eating ice cream by Cardiff Bay. "I was pretty lucky to be put in a flat in Talybont North with some pretty cool people," Heather told a fellow Cardiff student in a March

2022 video interview for the university's alumni network as part of Women's History Month. "There were five of us and we're still best mates now, which is amazing."

She loved the city when the Six Nations rugby union tournament was on. The streets became a sea of red banners and rugby shirts, whilst Welsh flags with a fierce red dragon on a green and white background were waved or draped over walls and windows.

Heather was in her second term at uni when she headed up to London to play in a university competition held at the famous Lord's Cricket Ground. Whilst there, an announcement rang out over the tannoy . . .

"Could Heather Knight please come to reception?"

"What have I done?" she thought. "Is it something to do with my car?"

Heather was given a telephone number and told to call Clare Connor, the head of England women's cricket. It turned out that celebrated batter-wicketkeeper Sarah Taylor had suffered an injury to her hip on England's tour of India and Heather had been called up to take her place. Wow!

Heather had to leave Lord's in her car, drive all the way back to Cardiff to pack, then drive back to London for an early-morning flight to India. In the frenzy, she managed to message her personal tutor at uni saying that she'd be back in a month! It was fortunate that her tutor was so keen on cricket.

Meanwhile, Clare Connor informed the media of the call-up. As the BBC reported in February 2010, she said, "Heather is a talented cricketer who scores huge runs at county level and I'm sure she will seize this chance to impress." Heather had plenty of time during the flight to think about what playing for England would feel like; she was nervous but excited.

India had already won the five match

ODI series 3–1 by the time Heather got to play. She was one of two debut players, the other being all-rounder Danni Wyatt, her teammate from the England Academy. On 1 March 2010, the pair stepped out onto the grass of the Bandra Kurla Complex in Mumbai. Heather couldn't quite believe it – she was playing for England! Not that there was much of a crowd present.

"There was probably one person there, and I think it was a parent [of one of the players]!" recalled Heather later, in her March 2020 BBC Sport blog. "No-one really took notice of what was going on."

India batted first with the legendary Harmanpreet Kaur compiling what looked a likely match-winning innings of 84. Heather didn't take any catches that day, and wasn't asked to bowl her off-spin. Danni Wyatt, on the other hand, got to bowl four overs and swooped to run out Amita Sharma late in the innings.

By that point in the game, the air pollution

in the city had become so bad that Heather felt herself overcome by the smog. In the same blog, Heather wrote, "I was starting to wheeze and cough, and I was thinking, 'How will I open the batting?!' But luckily it was fine."

England needed 207 to win and Heather began England's innings with Ebony Rainford-Brent (now a celebrated cricket commentator). She scored her first run in international cricket with a nudge for a single off her fifth ball. India were bowling tightly and Heather was finding it hard to score. After eight overs, she had just seven runs to her name and had lost her opening partner when Ebony was LBW to Rumeli Dhar for 17.

Her first four, in the ninth over, made her feel better. It was followed by five more fours as Heather got to grips with the Indian team's bowling.

In sight of a half-century in her very first innings for England, Heather was aware she wasn't scoring rapidly and needed to up the tempo. But then, disaster struck. She hit a ball bowled by medium pacer, Soniya Dabir . . . up it went to mid-off where Jhulan Goswami took an easy catch.

OUT!

Heather had made 49 runs from 101 balls. Her first innings for England had lasted two hours and two minutes, and taken England just over halfway to their target. Teammates took up the baton with three scoring 20s: Lydia Greenway, Laura Marsh, and Danni Wyatt who struck the winning runs. "Danni was as cool as a cucumber under pressure. It was so nice to share that moment with her," Heather reflected afterwards in her March 2020 BBC Sport blog.

Heather's trip to India, training and playing with the England squad left her wanting more. But first, there was her university degree to return to. In a Cardiff University blog in May 2017, she said, "I had to come back and throw myself into uni and catch up with everything. Life outside cricket helped me do better at cricket, though, because if cricket's everything, then that's a *lot* of pressure."

Heather's next two years at uni were a whirlwind of hard studying, hard cricket and lots of travel. She was called up on England tours to Sri Lanka, Australia, South Africa and New Zealand. Her Cardiff flatmates got used to her long absences but always welcomed her back.

Heather was at the end of her teens, but as she was often on tour for months at a time, she had to learn quickly to plan and manage her time like a seasoned pro. She achieved her academic goal, gaining a Bachelor of Science degree from Cardiff in 2012. Would she also achieve her cricketing goals?

⭐ CHAPTER 5 ⭐

Piling on the Runs

After her debut in India, Heather's second game involving England wasn't quite as exotic or memorable. For starters, it was held at a functional ground in Loughborough where the England team trained. And there was the small matter of Heather finding herself playing *against* England as part of an England A side (a sort of second team). To make matters worse, she was run out on six and had to sit and watch her opening partner, Caroline Atkins, blast 74.

Heather felt some distance away from becoming an England regular. She also had a vast amount of university course work to catch up on. But she threw herself into practising in the nets, working on her batting as well as games for Berkshire Women. She averaged an excellent 43.4 runs per innings for Berkshire in the 2010 Women's County Championship with a high score of 101 not out. It wasn't long before England came calling again.

Heather was added to the squad for a five-match ODI series versus New Zealand. She played well at times, okay at others, but couldn't quite get the big scores that would make her a definite England starter.

Still, she was thrilled to be picked that winter for England's tour of Sri Lanka, involving two ODIs and three T20 games. Unfortunately, the ODIs didn't go well. She was out for a duck (no runs) in the first match, and just as she was getting going on 15 not out in the second, down came heavy rain and play was abandoned. Frustrating.

At least, early the following year, she scored

her first half-century for England. It came against Australia, at Perth's WACA (Western Australian Cricket Association) ground during an ODI. She'd opened the innings with Danni Wyatt and managed to strike eight boundaries in her 72. Only her captain, Charlotte Edwards, outscored her with 90.

By this point, Heather considered herself a batter first and bowler second. She didn't even get to bowl for England until her 15th ODI, taking 0 for 10 off three overs. Three ODIs later, whilst playing at Potchefstroom in South Africa, she did take her first international wicket – that of South African captain, Cri-Zelda Brits. And in the ODI that followed, she took two wickets and scored 55 – a satisfying all-round performance.

When asked in an interview with charity the Female Lead in October 2016 about the best advice she had ever been given, Heather answered, "To trust yourself and never think that you've made it. Even when things are going well you should work that little bit harder to make sure it stays that way."

Heather kept on grafting at her game. She spent hours practising her stance, her shot timing and a range of different strokes so she could play shots all around the ground. She worked on her fielding and bowling too.

The hard work helped Heather have a brilliant domestic season, playing county matches in 2013. It started with a bang on 6 May when she made a blistering 153 not out against Middlesex. She scored 604 runs in the 2013 Women's County Championship at an incredible average of 100.66 runs per innings. Astonishing! She also scored 225 runs in the T20 County Championship at 56.25, a high average for T20 games. In mid-season, she felt in good form, which was just as well because . . . the Aussies were coming.

That year was the first time the Women's Ashes series was played under new multi-format rules. The competition involved a single Test match (worth six points to the winners), three ODIs (worth 2 points each) and three T20 games (also worth 2 points). The first team to reach ten points or more were the winners. Because Australia were defending champions, a draw meant they would keep the trophy.

The Test match at Wormsley began with Australia forging a good score of 331. Heather opened the batting in England's reply. She played well and England reached 80 for 1 before there was a big collapse . . .

Eighty for 2 became 84 for 3, then 97 for 4, and 102 for 5 when Tammy Beaumont was out. When Jenny Gunn also fell, England were reeling at 113–6, still more than 200 runs behind.

Thankfully, spinner Laura Marsh came in and stuck around. She played slowly and defensively, letting Heather take most of the scoring shots. By the end of the day's play, the crowd were on their feet cheering Heather off the field. She and Laura had survived – Laura on 13, she on 85. A sleepless night followed as Heather played the innings over and over in her mind. She was desperate to make her first hundred for England.

Next day, Heather and Laura continued where they'd left off. Laura eventually went on to make the slowest half-century in the history of women's Test cricket! It took her 291 balls. In contrast, Heather drove her 263rd ball, ran a single then jumped with joy. She had scored a hundred for England!

And on she batted . . . the Australian bowlers rarely troubled her and the runs kept mounting. But, with England getting close to Australia's score, Heather lost her wicket – she was run out by Aussie fielder, Rachael Haynes.

Heather trudged back to Wormsley's pavilion, with its straw thatched roof, exhausted but proud. Her 157 had taken her seven hours during which time she'd faced 338 balls.

It had been a masterpiece of concentration and technique.

England ended up making 314, close to Australia's score, and Heather contributed precisely half of the total. Her 157 placed her seventh on the list of England's biggest century makers – a list topped by the brilliant Betty Snowball who had made 189 against New Zealand all the way back in 1935.

As *Wisden* reported in June 2023, Heather's captain, Charlotte Edwards, was proud. "We were ready for Heather to come alive in international cricket, and that was her moment. It was an exceptional knock, and it made us realise what a player we had."

In her March 2020 BBC Sport blog, Heather described it as "the moment I felt like I belonged in an England shirt". Her only disappointment (besides not scoring a double hundred) was the game ending in a draw. But without Heather, England would have lost the

Test and given Australia a strong, six point start.

Charlotte and Heather's other teammates excelled themselves in the ODI and T20 series that followed the Test. Heather cracked a sparky 69 in the third ODI as England went into a 6–4 lead. England then managed to win all three T20s, defeating Australia 12–4.

Heather unfortunately suffered a hamstring injury in the last T20 game at the Riverside Ground near Durham. But it didn't stop her celebrating wildly with her triumphant teammates. In a June 2023 interview in *Wisden*, teammate Nat Sciver-Brunt said, "After we won, we wheeled Heather around the Riverside in a little groundsman's cart for a celebratory lap." Many of the players stayed up late and slept in their England kit that night.

However, having helped win the Ashes, Heather nearly lost them! In the buzz of celebrations and media events, somehow the Women's Ashes trophy had come home in her luggage. It stayed at her home for ten weeks before the English Cricket Board realised and asked for it back!

At the end of 2013, Heather found herself at a dinner in the famous Long Room at Lord's Cricket Ground. She was there to receive the Walter Lawrence Women's Award for the highest score in women's cricket (a trophy that Nat Sciver-Brunt, Tammy Beaumont and Heather again in 2019 would all win later). Hamstring injury apart, 2013 had been a phenomenal year for Heather.

★ CHAPTER 6 ★

Turning Pro

Heather entered 2014 in good spirits but with an uncertain future. Although now much more a part of the England set-up, making a career from cricket for a woman was tough. Even top players in the England team weren't paid to be full-time professionals.

In the past, it had been even worse. Female cricketers selected for England were not only unpaid or poorly paid, they also had to pay for their own England kit, and sew the badge onto their caps themselves. Many had to juggle other jobs with practising and playing cricket, pleading with their employers for time off or going on unpaid leave, all to play for their country.

Heather had no plans for a career outside of cricket. "If I hadn't become a cricketer, I don't know what I would be doing now except wishing I was one," she told the *Times* newspaper in November 2016. "It's always been cricket, one way or another."

She was fortunate that her parents were able to help her buy a flat, and in 2013 she gained a part-time contract to work as an ambassador in Wales for the Chance to Shine cricket charity. It was fun work helping to coach and inspire young female cricketers.

Heather and England managed to keep hold of the Ashes in 2014 by drawing the series in Australia. Then came the big news. The English Cricket Board decided to make their women's team professional by awarding 18 full-time contracts to elite players including Charlotte Edwards, Tammy Beaumont, Danni Wyatt and Heather. The sums the players were paid were

not on par with their male counterparts,
but it did give them some financial security.

"I don't think anybody expected it quite
so soon and it was amazing news when the
contracts came in," Heather told Sky Sports
in September 2014. "It's a massive step for us
and for women's sport as well. It makes a big
difference personally."

Interest in women's cricket was growing
and new opportunities occurred. After Heather
had impressed many Australians in the two
back-to-back Ashes series, she was offered
the chance to play for Tasmanian Roar in the
Women's National Cricket League in Australia. The
competition ran from October to January (through
the English winter when there was no cricket on at
home) and so she was delighted to take part. She
ended the season as the Roar's top scorer.

Heather returned to Tasmania the following
winter, but was also paid to captain the Hobart
Hurricanes in a brand new T20 competition – the

Women's Big Bash League (WBBL). Again, she made a big impact, bagging 363 runs, winning three player of the match awards and being voted the Hurricanes' most valuable player.

Women's cricket was booming and with it came new products and sponsorship deals. Heather was delighted to become involved with the design and launch of the UK's first ever range of women's cricket gear in 2015. She couldn't believe it when cricket equipment companies, SM and Cricket Deal Direct, chose to launch women's bats (slightly lighter than men's bats), pads and gloves – all under the name: the Heather Knight Cricket Collection.

Until then, many female players had to make do with kit designed for boys or men, which often didn't fit well. "I remember when I was playing Under-11s, wearing these massive pads and not being able to run! It's massively important to get kit that's right," Heather told the CRICKETher website in April 2015.

Heather rarely changes bats. She has a spare for use in the nets but for out in the middle in matches prefers to use the same bat for as long as possible. In contrast, she cannot wait to swap old, stinky batting gloves for a new set, often going through five or six pairs of gloves a summer.

Later in 2015, Heather swapped her batting gloves for cycling mitts as she took part in a gruelling 590-kilometre-long cycle ride – the PCA Big Bike Ride 2. It started at Truro in Cornwall, wound its way through her home county of Devon, then visited three county cricket grounds – Somerset, Hampshire and Sussex – before ending at a fourth, the Oval in London.

Among the 70 riders were cricketers Matt Coles, Rob Key (now director of the England men's team) and fast bowling legend, Darren Gough. Heather also had two of her teammates from the England squad for company – Lydia Greenway and Tammy Beaumont (or 'Mrs Bump' as she became known due to her habit of falling off her bike).

Not that Tammy was the only casualty. There were plenty of spills but none funnier than Matt Coles who slid off his bike and got covered in cow manure. Heather managed to stay in the saddle for the whole trip which raised more than £130,000 for charity.

It may have been, in Heather's words, "a seriously gruelling ride", but it was a breeze compared to the charity event she had been a part of the previous year . . .

CHAPTER 7

Climbing Mount Kili

"The time's 2am, the temperature's somewhere between –15 and –20°C and the final 1,000 metres of the tallest free-standing mountain in the world stands dauntingly in front of me . . . Welcome to the longest day of my life . . . Welcome to Mt Kili Madness." So wrote Heather in her Sky Sports Blog in October 2014. What on earth was she up to?

Heather wasn't on her own. She was part of a band of intrepid cricketers who had spent a week in Tanzania trekking to and then up the steep slopes of the magnificent Mount Kilimanjaro. This formidable snow-capped volcano stands

5,892 metres above sea level (more than four times higher than the UK's highest mountain, Ben Nevis). 'Kili' is the highest peak in Africa and a tough climb even for super-fit sportspeople.

Heather and 26 others donned their hiking boots and head torches to clamber up the volcano's craggy slopes. The party included South African fast bowling legend Makhaya Ntini, ex-England spin bowler Ashley Giles, along with England women's supremo all-rounder, Clare Connor.

As the group climbed higher and higher, the amount of oxygen in the air got less and less. This made even short walks incredibly tiring. Each night was spent trying to grab some sleep in a chilly, draughty tent. Despite being dog-tired from their efforts each day, Heather found it hard to sleep.

The idea for this caper came from hotel consultant David Harper, a keen cricket fan. He joked to his wife that the only way he was

going to play cricket at the highest level was
if he played at the top of a mountain. The
idea took hold and David organised the Mt Kili
Madness expedition. Its aim was to break the
world record for the highest altitude game of
cricket. The previous record holder was a game
played part of the way up Mount Everest –
5,165 metres above sea level.

Everyone who took part was raising money
for three charities: Cancer Research UK, Tusk
(a charity trying to stop the killing of elephants
for their ivory tusks) and the RCSF (Rwanda
Cricket Stadium Foundation, later renamed
Cricket Builds Hope), a charity close to Heather's
heart. The RCSF were striving to build Rwanda's
first cricket stadium and develop the game in
the country. Heather was a trustee of the charity.

Now, on the last night of the climb up
Kilimanjaro, Heather was wrapped up warm
and wearing a head torch. She and the others
walked single file up the gnarled volcanic rock

towards Kilimanjaro's summit. Heather reckoned the final march began in the middle of the night because no one wanted to see how steep and tough the route ahead was!

The conversation, which had been sparky and chirpy all week, died away. Everyone was tired and concentrating on putting one foot carefully in front of the other. For a while, Clare Connor's phone played music to keep them company, but then its battery died.

Sunrise brought some warmth. But it also lit up the path ahead and showed everyone how far they still had to go. Heather reckoned the last two hours were the hardest. Some of the trekkers, including Clare Connor, were feeling dizzy and sick. Heather had to help guide Clare to stop her from stumbling. Then, all of a sudden, they were there . . . on top of the 'Roof of Africa'.

The view was amazing and mind-numbing. Heather and the others felt relief and a great sense of achievement.

Everyone took a moment to take in what they could see. Then, they descended 50 metres down into the crater just below the peak, where they rolled out the portable pitch and put the stumps into place. The players were planning to play a 20 overs a side game under full T20 rules, but the clouds were already rolling in, so ten overs per team was decided upon.

Heather was captain of one team, the Gorillas, and Ashley Giles captained the other, the Rhinos. They picked their sides, despite the fact that several players were too exhausted to take part. Being able to stand up straight and not vomit was Heather's main guide to selecting teammates!

The Gorillas got an early boost when Heather won the coin toss. "I went for the old banker . . . runs on the board!" she exclaimed in her blog for Sky Sports in February 2015. "Bowling was difficult and running was near on impossible, but we managed it somehow."

With so little oxygen, players got dizzy and out of breath surprisingly quickly. Striking the ball though was a dream as the thin air meant a well-hit shot saw the ball rocket away. Luckily, the expedition had packed 24 orange-coloured balls for the game because quite a few were lost!

Heather managed to launch two BIG sixes that disappeared out of sight and ended up top-scoring for her team with 21 before being run out. The Gorillas ended their innings on 83 – a good total in ten overs.

Heather took the ball early on for an over of off-spin. Facing her was her rival captain, Ashley Giles. Although best known for his bowling, Ashley had scored over 5,300 runs in first class cricket, with a top score of 128 not out. That included 1,421 runs in Test matches for England. Heather needed to bowl well.

She turned and stepped up to the bowling crease . . .

Over came her bowling arm as she planted her front foot . . .

The ball whirled away and landed on the pitch. Ashley played a shot but the ball hit his pad.

"Howzat!" roared Heather's team. The umpire raised her finger. OUT! The Rhinos were 9 for 1.

By the end of the ten overs the Rhinos had lost nine wickets and scored 64 runs. Heather's team were the winners!

After brief celebrations, photos and last looks at the astonishing views, it was time to pack up all the kit and head down Kilimanjaro. Heather was now part of a world record breaking team. But the first thing she most wanted to do once at the bottom of Kilimanjaro was to take a hot shower.

"It was one of the toughest things I've ever done, but one of the best," she concluded on her Sky Sports blog. "To everyone involved in Mt Kili Madness, thank you and never again!"

The expedition raised thousands of pounds for the three charities and Heather has since returned to Rwanda to help out and coach girls getting into the game. Rwanda got its cricket ground – the Gahanga International Cricket Stadium – in 2017.

Five years later, the Rwandan women's team managed to qualify for the ICC Under-19 Women's T20 World Cup. Heather was delighted. At their first major tournament, the team played well. They reached the Super Sixes stage, defeating Zimbabwe and the West Indies along the way.

"Imagine what it means to a young girl in Rwanda to see her country on that stage," remarked Heather on the ECB (English Cricket Board) website in January 2023. "She'll know that she can aspire to something similar, and you can't put a price on what it means to inspire the next generation like that."

★ **CHAPTER 8** ★

Captaining Your Country

Long before Heather was born, pioneering female cricketers were battling hard for the right to play any sort of cricket. Before the Women's Cricket Association was formed in 1926, women's cricket matches were rare and mostly casual contests held on village greens. Sometimes, women had to play whilst jokes and heckles were made by ignorant men on the boundary.

Cricket's very first superstar, English batter W.G. Grace, wrote in 1899 that, "Cricket is not a game for women," and most men of the time agreed. At the time it was widely believed that a woman's place was in the home, cooking, cleaning and caring for children, not out working or playing energetic sports like cricket. Many schools even banned girls from playing cricket as they considered it 'unladylike'.

Forming at the start of the 20th century, the Suffragettes were an organisation dedicated to gaining the right for women to vote in elections. One of their leading lights was Helen Archdale, who was sent to jail for her protests. Her young daughter, Betty, later became England's first female cricket captain.

In 1934, Betty Archdale and her team boarded the SS *Cathay* liner at Tilbury Docks in London and began the 32-day ocean voyage to Australia to play the first ever women's Test match. Rather than being paid to play, each England player had to pay £80 to take part (equivalent to almost £5,000 today).

Betty's side won two and drew one of the three-match series with Australia. The sides continued to play each other but women's Tests were slow to catch on in many other countries. As of the start of 2024, the West Indies had played 12 Test matches, Pakistan three and Sri Lanka just one.

Women's international cricket has mostly focused on T20s and ODIs. The first ODI World Cup was for women not men, and cricket has another pioneering England captain – Rachael Heyhoe Flint – to thank for it. An England cricketer for 23 years and the first woman to hit a six in Test matches, Rachael convinced businessman Jack Hayward to fund the first Women's World Cup in 1973. The tournament, which ended with England winning the final and Rachael lifting the trophy, was such a success that a World Cup for men was hastily organised and held two years later.

Rachael passed away in 2017, but remains an icon of the game. Women's teams in England and Wales now compete for the Rachael Heyhoe Flint Trophy each year, alongside another competition, the Charlotte Edwards Cup. This is named after Heather's first England captain, to celebrate the impact she has made on the game.

Charlotte 'Lottie' Edwards became captain in 2005 and led England to three Ashes series wins and two World Cup triumphs. She played 309 matches for England and scored over 10,000 international runs – an incredible achievement.

Heather got on really well with the England captain. The pair had played together at Berkshire in county cricket and sometimes at club level for Wokingham Ridgeway. Heather would often ask Charlotte's advice and was delighted when she was made England vice-captain, under Charlotte, in 2014.

In a July 2015 interview, reported in the *Independent*, Heather was asked whether she'd like to be England captain herself. She answered, "It's something that I'd love to do. Hopefully, if given the chance, I could have a decent crack at it. But there are some decent candidates in the team, so who knows? Lottie could go on until she's in a wheelchair."

Charlotte led Heather and the rest of the England side into the 2016 T20 World Cup in India. England won all four of their group games but were knocked out by Australia in the semi-final.

New coach Mark Robinson wanted to make changes after the World Cup. Despite being the tournament's second-highest run-scorer, Charlotte was not selected and retired from international cricket. She is now in demand as a coach and commentator about the game.

Heather was appointed captain. She and her family were immensely proud; it was a great honour but also a huge responsibility. And how would England fare without Charlotte's runs, skills and vast experience? "It's going to be really challenging," Heather told the *Guardian* in June 2016. "It's hard to put into words her contribution on and off the pitch – she's been the leader for ten years and the dressing room will be very different [without her]."

Heather's first match in charge was an ODI at Grace Road, the county ground of Leicestershire. She felt nervous on the morning of the game but had lots to focus on once out in the middle. There were bowlers to choose, fielders to place and tactics to carry out. Pakistan started well and were on 93 for 3 until Heather introduced England's demon bowler in the 26th over . . . herself!

Out!

Iram Javed was caught by Lauren Winfield-Hill off Heather's second ball of the game.

Out!

Sidra Ameen mis-hit the ball, sending it back towards Heather who took a sharp catch.

Out!

It was another caught and bowled in Heather's next over. The opposing captain, Sana Mir, was gone and Pakistan were reeling at 115 for 6.

Out!

Heather brought herself back on late in
the innings and struck almost immediately.
Sania Khan was caught by Tammy Beaumont.

Out!

Two balls later and it was Kate Cross who
made the catch. Asmavia Iqbal was gone
and Pakistan were all out for 165. Heather had
a five-for. She'd taken five wickets for 26 runs:
brilliant bowling by the new England captain.

England made light work of their target,
getting their runs with more than 18 overs
left. Tammy Beaumont hit 70 and Heather an
unbeaten 50 to see England home. It made
her the first female player in an ODI to take five
wickets and score 50 runs. "I was dreaming of
a hundred on debut, getting a five-for never
crossed my mind," said Heather after the game,
reported by the BBC in June 2016. What a start
to her reign as captain.

Heather didn't have to wait long for her

second game in charge – she led England out the very next day, this time at the New Road ground in Worcester. "After the first game, everyone said it would be downhill from there," she noted in an interview with ESPNcricinfo in July 2016. "But our second game topped it."

England then went on the attack, with Lauren Winfield-Hill and Tammy Beaumont both making centuries. England's 378–5 remains the side's highest ever ODI total. A dumbstruck Heather told ESPNcricinfo, "I was sat there at lunch shaking my head thinking, 'I can't believe we just scored 380!' We hit 11 sixes!" England won by 212 runs.

Not all of her 160 games as England captain (as of March 2024: 7 Tests, 79 ODIs and 74 T20s) have gone so well since, but that hasn't stopped Heather from developing her own leadership style and skills. This includes learning how to keep players calm and confident in the middle of a match when under pressure – which requires getting to know new players better.

One interesting technique Heather uses is called 'feedback speed dating'. Heather sits down with a player for two minutes. She tells them one thing they have improved recently and one thing they still need to work on to do better. Then the player gets to assess Heather in the same way.

Heather knew from the start of her captaincy that she had to lead in her own way and not try to copy Charlotte. In return, Charlotte thinks she's done a fantastic job. Speaking on Sky Sports in June 2019, Charlotte praised Heather for the way she conducted herself and the way she performed. "Her game's gone up another level. She's not burdened by the captaincy."

⭐ CHAPTER 9 ⭐

World Cup Wonders

Months before the 2017 Women's World Cup, Heather and Clare Connor visited the world's oldest living Test cricketer. Eileen Ash (then Eileen Whelan) debuted in the first women's Test matches played in England in 1937. Eileen's remarkable life (1911–2021) included working for MI6 (the British Secret Intelligence Service) during World War II and playing golf until she was 98. Heather found her stories and scrapbooks about her time as a pioneering female cricketer fascinating and inspiring.

"I try to convey to the younger players the history of how we got where we are today.

We weren't given this on a plate," Heather told the *Sunday Times* later, in June 2019. "We want to remember where the game's come from. The women who fought for us to get where we are now as professional cricketers."

Whilst visiting, Heather joined Eileen in her weekly yoga session but couldn't keep up. "My pride, and a number of my muscle groups, are still in tatters after being put to shame by a 105-year-old," Heather wrote on her BBC Sport blog in February 2017.

Eileen never played for England at Lord's – the home of cricket. Women weren't allowed to play or be members at the time. Even today, women have yet to play a Test match at Lord's, although one is scheduled for 2026. *Finally!* So, the fact that Lord's would host the final of the Women's World Cup in 2017 was big news. "It's massively exciting," Heather told *Cardiff Connect*'s spring issue 2017 (Cardiff University's alumni magazine). "We'll be going into the tournament to be in that final at Lord's, and to win it . . . I don't think we'll be tournament favourites – but that suits us just fine."

After a training camp in Abu Dhabi followed by preparation at Loughborough, Heather's England squad were ready. But the tournament didn't start as Heather had hoped. They played India first and despite Heather making 46 and taking two wickets, England lost by 35 runs.

Heather's team rallied strongly. They made a record-breaking World Cup total of 377 in their second match, with Nat Sciver-Brunt scoring 137 runs and Heather 106. Heather was on a winning streak again in the next match, top-scoring with 82. In the fourth game, England made another monster total – 373. England's big batters like Heather, Nat and Tammy Beaumont were scoring freely and England notched six wins in a row, including a nail-biter versus Australia, which they won by just three runs.

England faced South Africa in the semi-final where Heather took the vital wicket of the dangerous Laura Wolvaardt. The game was a thriller and went down to the very last over. England pace bowler Anya Shrubsole clubbed a four with just two balls remaining to win the game. England were through to the final, but who would they face?

Two days later, England fans watched in shock as Indian batter Harmanpreet Kaur single-handedly demolished the Australians in the other semi-final. She scored a sensational 171 not out from only 115 balls. Her first fifty took 64 balls, her second 26, and her third an unbelievable 17 balls.

"She's hit seven sixes!"

"And 20 fours."

"She's dismantled the Aussie attack."

"And with an injured shoulder. Imagine if she'd been fully-fit!"

India were in the final for the first time since

2005 and were guaranteed plenty of noisy support at a sold-out Lord's. Having played many games in front of only a handful of people in the past, Heather was thrilled that 24,000 fans would be present. There were also around 200 million following the action on TV. Women's cricket had never been so well-supported.

A tradition at Lord's is the five-minute bell, rung just before the start of play. Heather was delighted to see it was Eileen Ash doing the honours for the final, but not so delighted when she was out for just one run. Nat Sciver-Brunt and Sarah Taylor scored good middle order runs whilst bowlers Katherine Sciver-Brunt and Jenni Gunn added 59 between them to take England to a total of 228. Would it be enough?

It was a match you couldn't turn your back on for a minute. In her first over, Anya Shrubsole smashed the Indian captain's stumps, but India fought back superbly. They passed the halfway mark to their target with Harmanpreet Kaur cruising. She reached her half-century untroubled. A run later, though, she hit a shot that flew high into the deep where it was caught by Tammy Beaumont. India were 138 for 3.

Heather shuffled her bowlers and fielders but India made it to 190 without losing any further wickets. They also had plenty of overs to chase down England's total. Things were getting desperate for England. Heather brought back her fiery fast bowler, Anya Shrubsole. Within five balls, Anya took a wicket. Then, Alex Hartley struck in the next over to make India 197 for 5.

Heather gazed round a full Lord's ground as Anya raced in the next over. The fast bowler cleverly changed her pace and angle to trick Veda Krishnamurthy into a poor shot.

OUT!

Two balls later, another rapid delivery from Anya speared through Jhulan Goswami's defences to rattle the stumps. India were now 201–7. The noise was deafening and the tension unbearable.

New batter Shikha Pandey set off for an unwise run and ended up losing her wicket. England fans celebrated raucously, but India were still 218 for 8, a mere 11 runs from victory. There were still two and a half overs to bowl. Which team would hold their nerve best?

Heather had thought about giving Anya a rest during her spell but instead kept her on. Anya charged in from the Pavilion End in the last-but-one over of the game. She took a wicket first ball. India were nine down.

Two balls later, Heather and the rest of the team thought they had won when Poonam Yadav skewed the ball up into the air. It was a simple catch . . . but Jenny Gunn dropped it. India scampered another run. Just ten needed now.

Anya bounded in again. She released

a searing delivery that crunched into Rajeshwari Gayakwad's off stump. Anya screamed with delight as she was mobbed by her teammates. India were all out for 219, having lost their last seven wickets for 28 runs.

The roar from the crowd was deafening.

"I can't even begin to describe the noise that went across Lord's when that final wicket fell," commented a tearful Ebony Rainford-Brent on BBC radio.

She wasn't the only one in tears. Some players were crying, others were laughing. Katherine Sciver-Brunt heckled her captain as she received the World Cup trophy, yelling, "We love you Heather!" The players were sprayed with champagne, the crowd cheered and fireworks went off, lighting up the London sky. It was chaos!

Heather somehow managed to keep her composure when interviewed after the game on the BBC's Test Match Special. "To win with some of my best mates, I'm absolutely delighted . . . What a tournament it has been. The support, the cricket and everything about it. Hopefully this can be a springboard for women's cricket in this country and around the world."

Heather's life was a whirl of media interviews and functions in the days that followed. Everyone wanted to congratulate her and the team. After a morning at the Oval cricket ground crammed full of interviews and posing for photos, Heather mislaid the World Cup for a panicky hour or two. What is it with Heather and cricket trophies?

It wasn't long before she was back to work, playing for Western Storm in the T20 Kia Super League in England, then leading England out for an Ashes series in Australia. Whilst there, Heather was awarded an OBE (Order of the British Empire) medal in the UK's New Year Honours list. Heather's teammates Anya and Tammy (the tournament's leading run-scorer) both received MBEs (Member of the British Empire).

"It's a bit surreal to be honest," Heather told Sky Sports in December 2017. "I think it's brilliant for women's cricket [. . .] Women's sport in general is in a really exciting place at the moment. It has created a real platform for it to go on to bigger things."

★ CHAPTER 10 ★

Trev's Tours

Elite international cricketers certainly clock up the air miles. A player in demand like Heather may easily spend more time away than at home each year. They may go on three, four or more foreign tours with their national team every 12 months. And that's just the start.

There might be further long spells away at a World Cup or another international tournament as well as playing in leagues like the Women's Big Bash League in Australia or the Women's Premier League in India.

Some players find being away from home difficult to handle. Heather accepts that it's part of being a top cricketer and is fortunate that family members sometimes fly out to spend time with her on tour.

Teammates provide Heather with lots of entertainment, and the England side she leads contains many close friends. Players like Tammy Beaumont, Nat Sciver-Brunt and Danni Wyatt have been playing together for more than ten years. Barbecues on the beach, silly challenges and bad shirt nights (where everyone has to parade the worst piece of clothing they own) all help add to the fun.

Sarah Taylor and spin bowler Sophie Ecclestone found one way of combatting boredom during downtime on long tours. They started buying and building LEGO® models! In 2019, Sophie bought Heather a LEGO® Technic™ boat to construct. Two years later, to celebrate the start of The Hundred (a new cricket competition in the UK), LEGO® figures of the various team captains were produced, including Heather.

Trev's Tours

As Sky Sports reported in July 2021, Heather was thrilled: "Who wouldn't be excited to see a LEGO® minifigure of themselves coming to life!"

As captain, Heather spends a lot of time talking to her teammates and coaches, and thinking about tactics and selection for upcoming games. On tours, it can be hard to switch off, but she strives to give herself some treats, including listening to podcasts, watching films and eating Japanese food.

Heather appreciates the opportunities that touring gives to see new places. "We're very lucky because we get to travel all over the world and go to loads of different countries to play cricket," she told charity the Female Lead charity in an online interview in October 2016.

Being curious about the world means that Heather always enjoys some sightseeing. She will often go on excursions to explore – from viewing incredible temples in India, to hiking through the volcanic landscapes

87

and hot springs of New Zealand. Sometimes she organises 'Trev's Tours' – day trips and sightseeing jaunts on rest days for the players.

"As a group, we know how privileged we are to play cricket around the world," noted Heather in her BBC Sport blog in April 2016, "and sometimes we get to meet some amazing people along the way."

There are experiences Heather would like to forget, though. Plunging into a tub full of ice after training is one of them! "There is absolutely nothing less fun than staring at a wall from the depths of an ice bath," Heather said in her BBC Sport blog in February 2016. So, when playing in Australia's 2016 Women's Big Bash League and given the chance to recover in the sea at Bondi Beach instead of an ice bath, Heather grabbed it. So did the rest of her Hobart Hurricanes teammates.

An added bonus came when they saw the beach's lifeguards being filmed for an Australian

TV show, *Bondi Rescue*. Heather and the others challenged some of the lifeguards to a game of beach cricket. "We had a pretty decent game, despite being interrupted a few times as they had to pop off to save a few tourists who had got into trouble in the sea!"

Whilst back in Tasmania with the Hurricanes, Heather and some of the other players took a boat to the remote Maria Island with just sleeping bags and food rations. "With no running water or electricity and a shark attack there a few months ago, the girls were a little dubious to say the least," wrote Heather in her BBC Sport blog in December 2015.

Heather wanted to hike and explore this rugged island and see its wildlife. This included wombats, kangaroos and the rare Tasmanian devil – although Heather was disappointed that it looked nothing like the TV cartoon character she remembered as a kid.

There was a moment of sudden chaos on this

trip when one of her teammates nearly stepped on a giant stingray while taking a dip in the sea. She said in her blog, "I've never seen the girls move so quickly!"

CHAPTER 11

In the Bubble

After scoring big runs at the Women's T20 World Cup in February 2020, Heather had a long wait for more international cricket. England didn't play a Test or ODI throughout the whole of 2020 because the UK, like elsewhere, was in the grip of the COVID-19 pandemic.

Within weeks of returning home from the World Cup, the country was in lockdown. To reduce the spread of the disease, people were not allowed to mix with others outside their households. At first, she quite enjoyed being at home and not travelling for a change. In an interview reported by the Women's

CricZone website in May 2020, she said,
"I feel like a retired old lady [. . .] Doing a bit
of gardening, cooking, going on long walks.
Definitely trying to get used to a very different
style of life."

But as time went on, Heather began to really
miss her cricket, the sense of competition and
time spent with her teammates. She tried to stay
fit and sharp, but it is hard training by yourself,
especially when you don't know quite what
you are training for and when it might occur.

The pandemic hit women's cricket especially
hard. Many series and competitions were
cancelled and lots of professional contracts for
players were withdrawn. Many female cricketers
didn't know when and where they would play
next. As captain of the England team, Heather
was involved in negotiations by video calls
about the pay cuts she and the other England
players had to take due to playing no cricket.

"As captain, you are used to being so busy,"

she told the *Times* newspaper in June 2020. "Then suddenly you're twiddling your thumbs, thinking, 'What have I got to do? What can I plan?' I'm a person that likes to be busy and working towards something. You suddenly realise, 'Who am I when I'm not England captain?'"

Fortunately, there were strong friendships throughout the England team and the players all tried to support one another. They kept in contact using video calls and apps, had fitness and running competitions over the internet and enjoyed a daily quiz organised by England batter, Sophia Dunkley.

Heather's brother Steve is a doctor, and many of her friends outside of cricket worked in the National Health Service (NHS), so she volunteered to help. She also produced a fun online exercise challenge mixing push-ups with a breakdancing move. This had her England teammates in stitches as Heather was widely regarded as the worst dancer in the side.

Like many people during the pandemic, lockdown gave Heather the chance to consider her future. As she told the *Times* in June 2020, "It's made me think about a world beyond sport, but also reinforced that I want to stay in sport – how much I enjoy helping shape decisions." She decided to enrol for another university degree: a masters in Leadership in Sport. "I'm not too sure where it will lead me," she said in a Professional Cricketers' Association press release in November 2021, "but I've really enjoyed doing it and learned a few snippets, which will be really useful for stuff on the pitch."

After months of lockdown, Heather and her teammates were thirsting for action. It finally came in September 2020 in the form of a five-match T20 series against the West Indies. Both teams had to enter a bio-secure bubble beforehand to prevent the spread of COVID-19. It meant the players lived in a hotel that was part of Derby's cricket ground.

In the Bubble

So, from no cricket, Heather went to almost too much cricket, with the ground being both the only thing she could see from her room and the only place she was allowed to walk around when going outside. Heather felt it was worth the sacrifice and knew the players should feel lucky. She thought these games might be the only women's live sport on in the UK that summer.

All five matches were played in an empty County Ground in Derby. It was an odd experience. No spectators were allowed in due to COVID-19 fears, so great moments such as Nat Sciver-Brunt's scorching 82 or West Indian Deandra Dottin's 100th six in international cricket were greeted in near silence; there was next-to-no-one there to applaud.

Heather scored 117 runs during the series, second only to Tammy Beaumont, and was pleased England won all five games. But she was especially grateful to the West Indies for flying in and taking part at short notice.

After just two days back at home and out of one bio-bubble, Heather was on the move again and heading into another. This time she was flying to Australia to play for the Sydney Thunder in the Women's Big Bash League.

Her first two weeks were spent alone in a hotel room as she endured quarantine. To help pass the time she propped a thick cushion up on her bed and practised throwing the ball into it. After quarantine, Heather and the others joined Australian players in one big bio-bubble. It was pretty intense, with all eight Big Bash teams living in the same place.

Heather had missed spectators being at matches so was thrilled that certain Big Bash games were letting them in. As an October 2020 article by ESPNcricinfo reported, she said, "I'm looking forward to having some fans in, and whether I'm booed or cheered, I'll just be happy to have some interaction and atmosphere."

After a couple of rained-off games, Heather got off to a rip-roaring start. She scored an incredible 83 from only 39 balls to guarantee victory against the Adelaide Strikers, followed by four more top-scoring games. It wasn't just her batting which made an impact. She helped see off the defending champions, the Brisbane Heat, taking three wickets – all in the same over. Epic!

The Thunder beat the Heat again in the semi-final, meaning Heather and Tammy Beaumont would face their good friend and England teammate Nat Sciver-Brunt, who was playing for the Melbourne Stars, in the final.

This match proved to be a tense, low-scoring affair. Heather's captain, Rachael Haynes, directed her bowlers brilliantly. With Nat out for 11, the Thunder reduced Melbourne to just 36 for four at the halfway stage. Then Rachael waved at Heather to come on to bowl her off-spin. The new batter was the dangerous Alana King, but she didn't last long.

Heather got her out and the Melbourne Stars limped to a final score of 86 for 8.

The Thunder were confident, but lost three quick wickets themselves. It took Heather and her captain to guide them home. As Alana King bowled the 13th over, Heather hit her for two runs, then a four, then finished the game in style with a massive six.

The Sydney Thunder were champions!

Heather finished the Women's Big Bash as one of its leading run-scorers. She had amassed 446 runs at a great average of 40.5 runs each time she batted. After the difficulties of lockdowns and bio-bubbles, Heather was jubilant. Little did she know that some of her toughest times were still to come . . .

★ CHAPTER 12 ★

Highs and Lows

As a top international cricketer for more than a decade, Heather was used to the ups and downs of the sport – but 2020–2022 were particularly tough.

New variants of the COVID-19 virus meant that there were yet more cricket cancellations and disruptions in 2021. The ICC Women's World Cup, supposed to be in 2021, was postponed to the following year. Other tours and competitions were cancelled as well.

England were able to organise a replacement tour to New Zealand when the World Cup would have been on. Heather oversaw a 2–1 series win in the ODIs and a 3–0 clean sweep in the T20s. In the return series in England in September that year, she hit two of her highest ODI scores, an 89 and then a marvellous 101, her second one-day century.

England played India at home, including a rare Test match in June. That game began promisingly but ended in frustrating fashion. England opened the batting and Heather came into bat at 79–1. She didn't hang around.

"Delightful way to get off the mark there by Heather Knight. Elegant drive through cover point," purred TV commentator, Charles Dagnall.

Heather ended up thumping a fabulous 95 in a shade under four hours. And with 68 from Tammy Beaumont, 74 from Sophia Dunkley and a spirited 44 biffed by Anya Shrubsole, England reached 396 before bowling India out for just 231 – a big lead.

A rare win in Women's Tests looked possible until rain got in the way. Lots of lost overs meant that this four-day game (men's Tests last up to five days) was a frustrating draw. Many women's Test matches end this way because of this four-day format.

Heather and other players would love to play more Tests and many would like to see them extended to five days. "Some of the best memories I have as a player have been in Test whites," she told the *Telegraph* in June 2022. "I'd certainly love to play more, as I know a lot of players do. When you grow up, you see Test cricket as the pinnacle."

England's next Test was six months away in Australia as part of the Ashes series. But COVID-19 again disrupted the team's preparation. Players had to isolate in their own bio-bubbles at home. They could not mix with other teammates and could only train with people they lived with. For England teammates and couple Nat and Katherine Sciver-Brunt, that was fine. But for many other young players it involved training with their with their parents. As the *Guardian* reported in January 2022, Heather outlined, "We've had mums feeding bowling machines, boyfriends slinging [the ball for batting practice] and dads batting. As you can imagine, it's been pretty comical but also not ideal preparation."

There were other changes, too. More COVID-19 restrictions meant the whole Ashes series was squeezed into just 19 days. In that time, three T20s, three ODIs and a four-day Test match had to be played. It gave the teams next-to-no time to recover after tough matches.

Australia pounced in the first T20 and won comfortably. They chased down England's score of 169 with nine wickets and three overs to spare. Frustratingly, the next two T20 games were rained off so England didn't get the chance to bounce back. Australia headed into the Test match 4–2 up.

In the Test, Australia scored 337. After their innings began, England quickly found themselves in trouble at 23 for 2. However, the Aussies hadn't contended with Heather at one of her favourite grounds, the Manuka Oval in Canberra before. She kept on going even as six further England wickets fell for just 56 runs. Heather belted a delivery from Ashleigh Gardner for a six, then hit a flurry of fours as she went past 50.

As Australia took more and more wickets, Heather remained defiant. She defended the many good deliveries that were bowled but punished the rest with firm clips, drives and cuts, often to the boundary.

With Heather on 92, England lost their eighth wicket for 168 runs. Out walked spin bowler Sophie Ecclestone. The England team room and the Manuka Oval stands were abuzz with chatter from staff, players and fans.

"Can Heather get her century?"

"Sophie's a good bat. She can hang around."

"We're still so far behind. We need a lot of runs."

"C'mon Trev, you can do it!"

Heather inched her way closer in singles

through the nineties, bringing up her hundred with a drive off the bowling of Alana King. It was a terrific century and Heather punched the air with delight.

Twenty-five overs later, she reached 150 with a powerful sweep shot that raced away for a four. Sophie was still there, having survived some close calls. She fell shortly afterwards, as did Kate Cross, leaving Heather to walk off the pitch undefeated, bat raised to applause. Heather had survived 294 balls to make 168 not out – almost 60 per cent of England's total of 297.

"A monumental effort from the England captain," spoke old teammate Ebony Rainford-Brent on TV commentary. "One of the finest knocks you'll see in Ashes cricket."

It wasn't the last of the drama.

The second innings unfolded with England chasing down a target of 257. On a pitch that was now playing tricks on batters, they responded well. Heather made a quickfire 48,

Nat Sciver-Brunt an equally rapid 58 and
Sophia Dunkley a sparkling 45 off just 32 balls.
England were 218 for 4, just 39 runs away from
victory when the wickets began tumbling . . .

224 for 5.

233 for 6.

236 for 7.

Everyone was getting excited *and* nervous.
Any result was possible.

With just three overs to go, three wickets
remaining and 13 runs needed, it looked like
bowlers Charlie Dean and Anya Shrubsole
would guide England home. But then Anya was
run out and Charlie was caught off the very
next ball. England were now 244 for 9. They had
lost six wickets for just 29 runs and were hanging
on by a thread.

Australia were firm favourites now, but
Kate Cross bravely batted out the last 12 balls
of the game. The match ended in a draw, but
a far from boring one. The result was in doubt

to the very last ball.

Despite the highs of her innings and the nail-bitingly close finish, Heather was desperately disappointed not to win the Test. But her team were still only 6–4 down with three ODIs to play. They were still in with a chance.

England, however, had a horror show in the three 50-over games. Their highest score was just 168 as they fell to some inspired bowling by Ellyse Perry, Annabel Sutherland, and Tahlia McGrath who, in the second ODI, took three wickets for just four runs. England were trounced 3–0 in the ODIs and lost the Ashes 12–4. That was hard to take.

The best way of getting over a tough loss is to turn the next match or series into a win. The 2022 English summer was absolutely stuffed full of cricket. There was the second season of The Hundred to enjoy, a series against South Africa, then the Commonwealth Games in Birmingham, which were to feature T20 cricket for the first time.

The thought of taking part and possibly winning a medal was enough to give Heather goosebumps.

Unlike some players, especially fast bowlers, Heather had suffered few long spells out with injuries. There had, of course, been strains, knocks and niggles along the way, and she'd taken some time out for her hamstring problem in 2013, but mostly she had been fortunate . . . until the summer of 2022.

Heather missed two T20 games against South Africa due to a hip problem. She had an injection in her hip shortly before England's first Commonwealth Games match, but it didn't help as much as she hoped. A scan confirmed that she needed an operation. "I needed a bit of fixing and a clean-out," she told reporters from ESPNcricinfo in August 2022.

It meant that she would miss not only the whole Commonwealth Games and The Hundred, but also the ODI and T20 series versus India that followed. Heather was gutted.

She had to hobble through many weeks of rehabilitation work after the operation. The good news was that the surgery was a success. Doctors thought it would not only stop the pain but also give her more movement in her hip joint, perfect for swivelling round when hitting pull and hook shots.

In the end, Heather's rehab took longer than she hoped and meant she also couldn't play in Australia's Women's Big Bash League that autumn. She missed five months of cricket and didn't return to action until England's tour of the West Indies in December. Heather was relieved – and thrilled – to be back.

CHAPTER 13

The Ashes is ON

It's not every day you get to see a 50-metre-high version of yourself and England men's captain Ben Stokes projected onto the famous Tower Bridge over the River Thames. But that's what happened to Heather at the start of June 2023.

The men's and women's Ashes series were both happening in the UK throughout June and July. It was the first time that the women's and men's fixtures were scheduled and promoted together and it saw women's cricket given much more attention than in the past. "This summer is going to be massive for women's cricket," Heather told the media at the start of June. "We really can't wait."

Matches were going to be played at major English grounds including Lord's, Edgbaston in Birmingham and Trent Bridge in Nottingham. It was an exciting time. "I'm really proud of how far cricket has come," Heather told the PA news agency in June 2023. "We've got more distance to go but this is a huge year for women's cricket and hopefully the scale of the Women's Ashes will help inspire a few more girls to come and watch us."

With Ben Stokes' team playing a fearless, entertaining style of the sport, interest in England cricket was really high. Heather wanted her side to be bold, too. And after watching England women's footballers win the UEFA European Championships the previous year, she was keen for her team to repeat the feat. "Watching the Lionesses was remarkable – we want a piece of that!" she told Ali Martin from the *Guardian* in January 2023.

Heather had never won a Test match as captain, but neither had she lost one! She'd been in charge of England for seven years yet had only got to captain the side in five Tests, all of which had ended in draws. Heather wasn't alone in her frustration. There are very few Test matches organised in women's cricket around the world; fewer than 50 have been played in total in the entire 21st century.

So, it was a real thrill when she led her team out at Trent Bridge – a ground she had never played on – for the 145th women's Test and the start of the 2023 Ashes.

Australia batted first with Ellyse Perry in scintillating form. She'd struck 99 when she was caught by Nat Sciver-Brunt. Ellyse's innings was eclipsed by Annabel Sutherland. Coming in as the number eight batter, she frustrated Heather's team; England simply couldn't find a way to get her out. Annabel's 137 boosted Australia's total to 473 – a formidable first innings.

Heather wasn't downcast. England's warm-up game the previous week had been against Australia A at Derby and they had scored an incredible 650, with Tammy Beaumont playing a monster innings of 201! Heather herself had scored 72. The runs would come.

Heather was right. Tammy started playing an innings that went from good . . . to great . . . to sensational. Heather and Tammy put on 115 runs together before the captain was out for a half century. Tammy went on and on to become the first English woman to score a Test double century. Her 208 off of 331 balls saw England reach a total of 463, just ten runs behind their rivals.

If the first innings were pretty much even, then it all went awry in the second innings. It started well enough with England's best spinner, Sophie Ecclestone, taking five wickets as Australia were all out for 257. A target of 268 for a famous win seemed gettable, but the pitch was getting harder to play on and one Australian bowled especially well. Ash Gardner spun out three of England's top batters in Heather, Tammy and Nat.

Then she took a further five wickets to finish with incredible figures of 8 for 66.

Australia had scored the first blow in the Ashes by winning the Test. Australia 4, England 0.

A 4–0 lead became 6–0 when Australia won the first T20 match at Edgbaston. Roared on by a noisy crowd, England had made 156 – a good score – only for Australia to pass their total with just one ball to spare. It was a thrilling game in front of a 19,527-strong crowd.

As Sky Sports reported in July 2023, Heather was positive after the game, saying, "We are getting closer and I am really proud" – but her captaincy was criticised by some cricket reporters. They singled out her decision to bowl England's world-class spinner Sophie Ecclestone in the last over rather than earlier in the innings. England now had to win every one of the last five matches to regain the Ashes. Few gave them any chance against the number one side in the world, but Heather hadn't given up . . .

CHAPTER 14

A Mighty Comeback

England regrouped in London four days later. Whereas some of her first England games had been watched by one or two hundred fans, over 20,000 were crammed into the Oval. They saw England pile on a big score – 186 for 9, with Danni Wyatt striking 76. It was the second highest total ever against Australia in a T20 match.

Australia nearly matched England and Heather had to cleverly juggle her bowlers and fielders. She still used Sophie Ecclestone to bowl the last over, but this time England won by three runs. Phew! Any win against the Aussies was to be cherished, especially in front of such a big crowd.

"We really felt the support and people on our side," said Heather in her post-match interview.

The teams made a short trip across London to play the deciding T20 match, at Lord's. More than 21,000 spectators witnessed yet another close game, with Australia starting strong but England roaring back. Eighteen-year-old Alice Capsey in particular was fearless, smashing two sixes and four fours in an innings that helped England win with just four balls remaining.

Heather's team had beaten Australia in a T20 series for the first time since 2017. And the Ashes series scoreline was narrowing: 6–4 now with all to play for. Over in the men's competition, a similar chain of events was occurring. Australia had won the first two Test matches, but England had bounced back with a stirring victory at Headingley and were on top in the fourth Test at Old Trafford before rain turned it into a draw.

The women's teams headed west to play at the Bristol County Ground four days later, for the first ODI. Australia won the toss and chose to bat. When their captain Alyssa Healy was out for just eight, England fans got excited. Could an Aussie collapse be on?

Nope. Australia rallied and posted a good score of 263 for 8. Beth Mooney top-scored with 81.

The England batters started off well, with Alice Capsey and Tammy Beaumont both getting into the 40s. But when Tammy was out in the 13th over, England needed a captain's innings to give them a chance. Heather hadn't scored heavily in the Ashes series so far. Now was her time to shine.

She started slowly, scoring just seven off her first 17 balls. England fans' hearts leapt to their mouths when Australia appealed for her out, LBW (leg before wicket), and called for a review. The wait for the decision on the big screen was unbearable!

"This is taking forever . . ."

"I can't bear the tension."

"Remember, the Aussies have won 15 ODIs

in a row . . ."

"If Heather's out, I think we're done."

After what seemed like an age, the scoreboard flashed into life . . .

NOT OUT

The roar from the crowd proved beyond doubt that most fans in the ground were rooting for England.

Heather continued batting calmly, scoring lots of ones and twos as wickets fell around her. It wasn't until the 30th over that she struck a boundary, sweeping a ball from Tahlia McGrath for four. She hit four more and a big six off of Ash Gardner as England, now eight wickets down, edged towards Australia's score.

Thirty-five overs after Heather had come in to bat, England and Australia's scores were level. Jess Jonassen bowled a loose delivery that reached Heather as a full toss (without bouncing on the ground first). The England captain responded by slapping the ball powerfully through the covers for her sixth four of the innings, and claiming the win.

"Yessssssss!"

You could hear her deafening yell on TV and around the ground as she was hugged by her batting partner, Kate Cross.

"The scream, the celebration, the Ashes remain alive," exclaimed commentator Charles Dagnall on TV. "From a seemingly impossible 6–0 down, England have dragged it back to 6–6!"

Heather's 75 not out had kept the series alive. It had also seen her pass 6,000 runs in international cricket for England. Amazing! Instead of focusing on her achievements, she typically talked about her team in the post-match interview. "The fight in the side is remarkable," she marvelled. "We've kept calm in the big moments. We've got a lot of momentum. The support from the crowd was unreal again. It has really made the difference for us."

Women's cricket was all over the news and the public couldn't wait for the next ODI, this time held at the Rose Bowl in Southampton. Hopes were high for another thriller. The match didn't disappoint.

After seven hours of enthralling, edge-of-the-seat cricket, it came down to the final ball of England's innings as they chased down Australia's big total of 282. In the dressing room, after getting out for 12, the captain wasn't her usual cool and calm self. Her friend and long-time teammate, Nat Sciver-Brunt, had played a stunning innings and reached 111. Nat was facing the last ball. She needed to hit a four to take the game to a tie-breaking Super Over, or a six to win.

Some fans in the stands had their hands over their eyes. The tension was unbelievable. Nat swung hard but could only manage a single down the ground. Australia had won by the small

A Mighty Comeback

margin of three runs and retained the Ashes.

Heather, her teammates and the fans were all gutted. There were spells of gloomy silence on the team coach as it left the Rose Bowl. The ODI series was tied 1–1, and no side had defeated Alyssa Healy, Ellyse Perry and the rest of the Australian juggernaut in an ODI series for ten years. Some teams thought they were invincible and almost gave up before a ball was bowled. Not Heather's team!

She reminded her players how closely-fought the games had been. England were close to matching Australia. They just needed to put together one more stirring performance, this time at Taunton in Somerset, a ground Heather knew well from her time playing for Western Storm.

This time, England batted first but things didn't start well. Ashleigh Gardner had Sophia Dunkley caught in the third over, whilst Megan Schutt smashed Tammy Beaumont's stumps in the fourth. England were 12 for 2 and in real trouble.

Heather joined Nat Sciver-Brunt at the crease. The pair needed to rebuild, and fast!

In the 24th over, Nat reached her 21st 50 in ODIs and Heather smashed the ball down the ground for a six, just a couple of runs behind her partner. Two balls into the next over and Heather tickled a ball round the corner to bring up her fifth four of the innings and her 26th ODI half-century. The crowd cheered.

Heather eventually fell for 67 but the 147 precious runs the pair had put on together was the highest England partnership against Australia in an ODI. Nat went on to make her second century in a row and England's total of 285 was just too stiff for Australia to reach. England had won the ODI series 2–1.

The Ashes ended: England 8, Australia 8. Heather's side had won over thousands of new fans with their skill and tenacity. They'd also earned the respect of their illustrious opponents. "I haven't seen a tighter series between these two, it's been outstanding. England should be very, very proud," said former Australian women's batter, Alex Blackwell on the BBC's Test Match Special.

"England have played a pretty fearless brand of cricket," noted Australia's player of the series, Ash Gardner, in her post match interview.

Speaking in an interview straight after the last match, Heather was tired, but said, "I'm hugely pleased. We've got two trophies against the world champions, which is pretty special. After the Rose Bowl it was a pretty quiet bus journey, so credit to the staff and the group for the way they've turned it around."

Over four times as many people attended games compared to the last Ashes series in England in 2019. The 23,207 fans who turned up for the Trent Bridge Test match alone broke the previous record by more than 8,000. Fans loved the high levels of skill, commitment and the exciting games the series generated. Millions more followed the drama on TV or the internet.

England may not have won the series but they'd gained bags of attention, interest and many new women's cricket fans. And that mattered to Heather in what was proving to be a big year . . .

★ CHAPTER 15 ★

Getting Equal

Aside from the Ashes, 2023 was an important year for women's cricket because small but positive steps were taken to making the women's game more equal with the men's. Heather saw many of the changes close-up, starting in the spring with the launch of the first ever Women's Premier League.

The Indian Premier League (IPL) is the richest cricket tournament in the world. Each of its ten teams bid at auction for home-grown and top foreign male players, and pay huge money for the best T20 cricketers. In 2017, for example, Rising Pune Supergiant bought Ben Stokes for £1.7 million. For the 2024 season, Mitchell Starc was signed by Kolkata Knight Riders for even more – a cool £2.35 million.

Small scale trials of a women's version of the IPL had been tried before, but in 2023, a fully professional Women's Premier League was launched. It contained five teams: Delhi Capitals, UP Warriorz, Gujarat Giants, Mumbai Indians and Royal Challengers Bangalore.

Heather was at the 2023 T20 World Cup in South Africa in February when the first WPL player auction was held. The team were actually playing Ireland in a group game at Paarl. Heather left it up to each player to decide if they wanted to follow the early stages of the auction before play. She resolutely set her own mobile to quiet mode and popped headphones in her ears so she couldn't hear any chatter. She didn't want any distractions before a World Cup match.

After the game, which England won comfortably (with Alice Capsey scoring England's fastest ever T20 50 in a mere 21 balls) the players returned to their dressing room. Phones started ringing and buzzing. Alice had been signed by Delhi Capitals for £75,000, Sophia Dunkley by Gujarat Giants for £60,000, and Sophie Ecclestone by UP Warriorz for a massive £160,000.

Whilst these sums are smaller than those paid at the IPL auction, they were a start at least for female cricketers who still earn far less than top male players. So, when Nat Sciver-Brunt went for a whopping £320,000, it attracted headlines around the world. Heather wasn't surprised at Mumbai Indians paying so much for her teammate. As the *Cricketer* reported in February 2023, Heather said, "She's one of the best cricketers in the world [. . .] I'm super-glad she's on our team."

A number of England players had entered the auction but not been bought. Heather believed she was one of them. She was just thinking about how she should console the other unsigned players in her team when she learned she had been signed by Royal Challengers Bangalore (RCB). She was going to the Women's Premier League!

Within ten days of England's last World Cup game, Heather found herself in the Indian city of Mumbai playing her first game in the WPL. She performed well, scoring 34 runs and becoming the only RCB bowler to take wickets as they went down to Delhi Capitals.

Heather's team played again the next day as the whole 22-game tournament was crammed into March. It brought Heather face-to-face with Nat Sciver-Brunt on the opposing side again. It wasn't the only unusual experience she had. Not being captain was another (RCB was captained by Indian star, Smriti Mandhana), as was playing in the same team as legendary Aussie all-rounder, Ellyse Perry and New Zealand run machine, Sophie Devine.

After the first two games, Heather enjoyed participating in the Hindu festival of Holi with her teammates. Holi celebrates the arrival of spring and revellers are covered in bright powder paints thrown in the air. Heather found herself plastered from head to toe in coloured powder.

She took to Twitter (now X) to ask her followers, "Anyone know how to get pink Holi powder out of blonde hair? Asking for a friend . . ." It didn't take long for England teammate Kate Cross to reply, "Shave it!" Not quite the answer Heather was looking for.

Despite her team not reaching the final, Heather loved the WPL. She'd been told there would be big crowds but couldn't quite believe the thousands she saw. Some games attracted 15,000–20,000 fans. One group game saw 30,000 spectators attend. Amazing.

"The cricket was at a really high standard and the crowds were unbelievable," Heather told the 100% Cricket podcast in April 2023. "I don't think I really appreciated the reach that the tournament was going to have. Cricket in India just breaks through popular culture."

Heather's hopeful that the WPL will grow and gain more teams. That will give many more female cricketers a chance of making a good living and may inspire other countries to start professional women's leagues as well.

May 2023 saw Heather back in England and in action for Western Storm in two competitions before taking part in an epic Ashes contest against Australia in June and July. Any possibility of a well-earned summer break after that? Not a chance. In less than a fortnight after the Ashes ended, Heather was captaining London Spirit in the third season of The Hundred. In her first match in the 2023 competition, she top-scored with 44 in just 27 balls against the eventual champions, Southern Brave.

With just 100 balls faced per team, each game in The Hundred is fast and furious. The 2023 edition, featuring eight franchises each fielding a men's and a women's team, was seen as a big success, especially for women's cricket. Crowds were larger than previous years and well-entertained with lots of close matches. Sadly, a few games were rained off – but that's typical of the English and Welsh summer!

The Hundred aimed to give the women's team equal billing to the men's. Many games were arranged as double-headers with the men's and women's matches played at the same ground, on the same day. Fans could then easily support both teams.

Thousands of people who'd never been to a game of women's cricket found themselves revelling in the action. Top overseas players like Marizanne Kapp, Sophie Devine, Smriti Mandhana and West Indian legend Deandra Dottin added to the glamour. Although, Heather was pleased to note, in the tournament final it was two of her England teammates, Danni Wyatt with a quickfire 59 and Kate Cross with three wickets, who won the game for Southern Brave.

Shortly before The Hundred began, Heather was invited to become a member of the MCC World Cricket Committee. This elite group of top cricketers and umpires includes greats of the game, such as Sri Lankan batter Kumar Sangakkara ex-Indian captain Sourav Ganguly, and former England captains Eoin Morgan and Clare Connor. The committee debates how cricket can develop and improve worldwide.

By now, Heather had completed her Leadership in Sports university degree and had been made Vice Chair of the Professional Cricketers Association (PCA). This organisation represents all professional cricketers in the UK, male and female. It aims to look after players during and after their playing career.

She also contributed to a special report called 'Holding Up a Mirror to Cricket', which came out in the summer of 2023. It heavily criticised those who run cricket in England, accusing them of unfairness. The criticisms included how female players were paid just a quarter of the match fee male players received for playing in an ODI game. For Tests, the match fee for women was even lower – just 15 per cent of the men's.

The England Cricket Board responded and in August 2023 increased England women's match fees to equal the men's. "It's another really good step forward for the game," Heather told PA news agency in August 2023.

Despite having a bigger role in how cricket is run off the field, Heather shows no signs of slowing down on the field. She's still totally committed to leading England in all formats, choosing not to play in the 2024 Women's Premier League so that she could captain England on their tour of New Zealand.

But when she retires, don't bet against her becoming even more involved in running the sport she loves. If she does, she will be following in the footsteps of previous England women's captains like Clare Connor and Charlotte Edwards.

From no changing rooms, crowds or professional cricketers, women's cricket has certainly come a long way since Heather first picked up a bat and ball with her brother to ruin their parents' garden furniture.

"I've always said I wanted to leave the game in a better position than when I started," Heather stated in the Professional Cricketers' Association's *Beyond the Boundaries* magazine in June 2023. "It is remarkable how things have progressed.

"I wish I was a youngster getting into cricket now. There's no better time to be a girl or woman playing cricket."

Heather Knight Fact File

(as of April 2024)

Born: 26/12/1990, Rochdale, England

Tests

12 matches

803 runs, 7 wickets, 12 catches

2 hundreds, 4 fifties, 94 fours, 2 sixes

Bowling average: 23.71

ODIs

137 matches

3,845 runs, 56 wickets, 43 catches

2 hundreds, 26 fifties, 369 fours, 20 sixes

Bowling average: 24.91

T20 Internationals

112 matches

1,923 runs, 21 wickets, 31 catches

1 hundred, 7 fifties, 198 fours, 34 sixes

Bowling average: 27.19

Read more sports books from Red Shed!

Amazing Cricket Stars

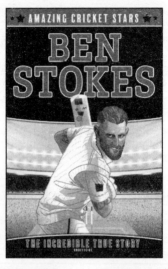

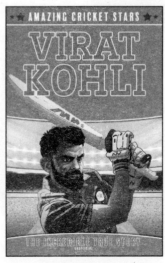

Incredible Sports Stories

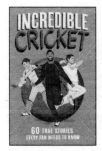   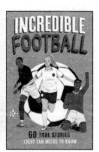

Amazing Football Facts

About the Author

CLIVE GIFFORD is an award-winning author
of more than 200 books, including the official
guide to the ICC Cricket World Cup 2019.
His books have won the Blue Peter Children's
Book Award, the Royal Society Young People's
Book Prize, the School Library Association's
Information Book Award and Smithsonian
Museum's Notable Books For Children.
Clive lives in Manchester within a short walk
of Lancashire's Old Trafford cricket ground.

Read on for an extract from
Amazing Cricket Stars: Mitchell Starc

⭐ CHAPTER 1 ⭐

Fast and Furious

Sunday, 15 November 2015.

"Say, this is one dangerous man!" exclaimed cricket commentator Mark Nicholas, as Mitchell Aaron Starc took yet another wicket for Australia.

Mitchell was playing for Australia on day three of the second Trans-Tasman Test against New Zealand at the WACA (Western Australian Cricket Association) ground in Perth. Fast, bouncy and often rock-hard, the pitches at the WACA have a fearsome reputation for being deadly for batters. So too, did Mitch!

Although he was only 25 years old and still

relatively new to international cricket, Mitch had already taken over 200 wickets for Australia in Tests, One Day Internationals (ODIs) and Twenty20 (T20) games. He was an exciting left-arm fast bowler, sometimes a little wayward, often quick and hostile, and always watchable. He was famous for his yorker – a ball aimed to pitch full (near the batter's feet) and hit the stumps or pads, to get batters out leg before wicket (LBW).

Australia had scored 559. Mitch had contributed precisely zero to the score. Normally, a good lower order batter, he'd been outfoxed by spinner Mark Craig and hit the ball straight up into the air to be caught easily. Craig took three wickets in that over but couldn't stem the Aussie tide of runs.

In the previous Test match, Mark Craig had frustrated Mitch . . . a lot. Craig and Trent Boult were the last pair of New Zealand batters and

Australia expected to get them out quickly to win the game. But the pair stuck around for 49 balls, scoring 46 runs.

After Craig had hit him for three fours, Mitch reacted. He retrieved the ball, spun and threw a wild throw in the batter's general direction. It missed Craig and raced away to the boundary, giving New Zealand four runs for free. Australia eventually won, but Mitch was given a serious telling off by match referee Roshan Mahanama and fined half of his match fee for his actions.

Off the pitch, Mitch Starc was polite, modest and made good friends with cricketers in other teams. But something clicked as soon as he walked onto a cricket ground, and he became extremely competitive. Earlier that year, he'd been given a warning for yelling in the face of Indian batter Murali Vijay after bowling him out.

Fast and Furious

In this second Test, New Zealand were motoring at 332 for two. Despite having already bowled 16 overs, Australia needed another fiery spell from Mitch.

Speed guns in the stadium measured the pace of balls bowled. Mitch began his new spell bowling just above 140 kilometres per hour – reasonably rapid – and he troubled both batters with his pace and swing.

A gentle wind – known as the Freemantle Doctor – blew in off the nearby Swan river as Mitch strode back to his bowling mark and turned to run in.

"C'mon, Mitch – crank it up!" yelled a teammate in encouragement. Mitch obliged. By his fourth over, he was bowling rockets!

Most of his deliveries were over 150 kilometres per hour – that's fast and gives batters so little time to react.

Mitch's first delivery to Brendon McCullum caught his bat and flew over the slips. The second, even faster, also clipped Brendon's bat and whizzed towards Mitch's teammate Nathan Lyon, fielding at second slip. Such was its speed, Nathan couldn't get his hands into position in time and the chance was dropped.

Mitch was annoyed, but tried not to show it to his teammates. Instead, he channelled his fury into bounding in even quicker. The last ball of the over zoomed towards McCullum at almost 155 kilometres per hour. It crashed into McCullum's bat and a chunk of wood exploded away. Mitch had broken Brendon's bat! A replacement had to be brought out.

The crowd were loving this.

"One hundred and fifty-five kilometres per hour? That's super quick!"

END OF SAMPLE